Pinot Noir
Arou[illegible]orld

Anne Krebiehl MW

IW&FS

The International Wine & Food Society

This Monograph – the twenty-third in the series – is
published in 2023 by
The International Wine & Food Society Ltd,
under the chairmanship of Michael Tamburri.

ISBN 978-0-900813-11-5

The International Wine & Food Society Ltd
4 St James's Square, London SW1Y 4JU, UK
www.iwfs.org +44(0)20 7827 5732

Commissioned by Andrea Warren
Edited by Katie Wyartt
Designed by Jayne Clementson
Printed in the UK by All Things Print, CO6 1RY

Contents

Photograph © Bodega Chacra

Introduction

"Qui bon vin boit, dieu voit"
(Those who drink good wine see God) – French proverb

What is it about Pinot Noir that captivates us so much? What is within us that responds so viscerally, so emotionally to wines made from this particular grape variety? It is a fascination that goes beyond mere alcohol; it is an intoxication of another kind.

Pinot Noir is not a grape for everyone. Some look down on it because its thinner skin means less colour, less body, less muscle in the finished wine, but the rest of us delight in its shimmering translucency and beguiling perfume. It cannot be pinned down and comes in myriad expressions, yet there is an undeniable and essential 'Pinotness' about it that haunts us – whether it has been caressed by Tasman breezes, shrouded in Pacific fog or whipped by Patagonian winds.

It speaks of its provenance, whether it has roots in Jurassic limestone, ancient schist or fractured slate; sometimes it comes with the scent of local wild thyme, pennyroyal, conifer or eucalypt that grow in its vicinity. It can channel tart cranberry, crunchy pomegranate, tender raspberry, juicy cherry and intense elderberry. With age, hints of undergrowth and truffle appear.

> **Pinot Noir captivates us, and its best examples transcend mere taste and flavour and let us glimpse something almost divine**

Elsewhere I once wrote that "there is something primordial in Pinot Noir's perfume, something earthy and eternal, something that

Photograph © Deutsches Weininstitut

encapsulates both life and death in its autumnal shades of decay. It can be a floral cloud of hawthorn blossom and tart, red fruit; it often is a deeply fruited sense of soil with dimensions of tea leaf, rock and forest; in its maturity it becomes a metaphor for dimming light, spent foliage and fading voluptuousness". In short, it captivates us, and its best examples transcend mere taste and flavour and let us glimpse something almost divine.

For some reason, Pinot Noir engenders obsessiveness, both in those who drink it and in those who grow and make it. Why? Is it because Pinot Noir is said to express what other wines cannot, something profound that is a link to a particular place and time? Because growing and making it is such a challenge? Because it excels when it has had to struggle? Or perhaps because it has been with us humans for such a long time, and has helped and nurtured us as we helped and nurtured it?

Whatever it is that makes it so fascinating to us, Pinot Noir has conquered the world, and this monograph charts its presence around the globe.

Chapter 1
Setting the scene

Scientists believe that Pinot Noir is about 2,000 years old but its origins are lost in the mists of time. While Pinot itself is a parent to numerous grape varieties, like Aligoté, Chardonnay and Gamay for instance, to date, nobody has been able to establish its parentage. As Jancis Robinson, Julia Harding and José Vouillamoz explain in their seminal book *Wine Grapes*, if analysed by eight standard DNA markers, Pinot Noir, Pinot Gris, Pinot Blanc, Pinot Meunier and Pinot Noir Précoce are identical – but analysis of more than 100 DNA markers shows genetic

Pinot Noir vine, Burgundy

Photograph © BIVB / Jean-Louis Bernuy

differences. These differences also explain clonal variations (see p73 for more on clones).

What is clear is that Pinot Noir emerged in a cool to temperate climate where its aromas could develop slowly, as Robinson *et al* note: "In hot climates it ripens too quickly and the relatively thin-skinned berries tend to shrivel."

Pinot Noir's thin grape skins explain two things. First, its susceptibility to rot and mildew to which it owes its reputation of trickiness and diva-like behaviour – as well as its nickname, 'the heartbreak grape'. Second, thin grape skins translate into relatively light colour and mouthfeel. Pinot Noir's tannins are never mouth-puckering like those of Cabernet Sauvignon.

While riper Pinot Noir tannins can be as lush as velvet, Pinot Noir tannins can be likened to the textures of starched Atlas silk via silk satin to silk chiffon, as tender as a caress. Certain clones and selections might be capable of delivering generous yields, but the wines they result in are uninspiring. Pinot Noir is best when its yields are restricted; it has never performed well as a workhorse grape.

Pinot Noir does best in cooler and temperate climates, as Oregon Pinot pioneer David Lett wrote (in an essay from 1996): "God never intended Pinot Noir to be a deeply coloured wine and indeed it rarely is if grown in the cool climates that allow full expression of the fruit's varietal character." Nonetheless, it thrives in a range of climates – in California's warm Russian River Valley, in cool England and many places in between.

Chapter 2
Pinot Noir's ascendancy in Burgundy

Pinot Noir has variously been called Morillon, Noirien, Auvernat – and more – in its long history. The first mentions of the term Pinot appear in the early 14th century – in Burgundy, of course. From the 5th century onwards, abbeys and monasteries were founded in Burgundy and were soon endowed with land by the nobility – either with vineyards or with land that could be cleared for vines.

Vines had been present in Burgundy since Gallo-Roman times. Several historians have tried to trace the advent and ascent of Pinot Noir in the region during these early centuries when people clearly grew grapes, and made and drank wine, but never named grape varieties.

None has done this better than Robert J Boidron in his invaluable book *Le livre du pinot noir*. What transpires is that Pinot, or its predecessors, were referred to variously as "*fin cépage, plant fin, noirien, bon plant, cépage roi...*" – so it must have stood out for its quality next to the less noble vines that made more common wines.

This is key, because, he writes: "Due to Pinot's limited ability to provide sufficient economic returns and achieve commensurate prices (when the wines could be marketed), the cultivation of this noble vine for many centuries remained in the hands of owners of revered estates (abbeys, episcopal properties, priories, etc) or of lands dependent on chatelains or other owners of Medieval fiefs. The wines were therefore reserved primarily for the purposes of worship, for consumption by the monks but also for the good tables of the wealthy, whether they were rich owners, merchants or crowned heads."

This means that there already was viticulture, there was land donated either to religious communities or owned by the aristocracy, and there were brothers and sisters, monks and nuns, to tend the vines as Burgundy emerged from the Gallo-Roman period into the Early Middle Ages from the 5th to the 10th centuries. This feudal society allowed Burgundy to become the birthplace of single-site viticulture. Let us evoke this period: wine is one of the most precious things, its importance elevated by its use initially in pagan and then Christian rites. There is no science, only faith and feudal rule; there are few creature comforts. Life is hard, hunger is real, so is misery. Wine is one of the few things that alleviates, that nourishes more than the body alone.

The Abbey of Cîteaux, between Dijon and Beaune

Monks tending the vines in Burgundy

Photograph © Bibliotheque Municipale de Dijon

The brothers and sisters who tended these ancient vineyards knew where snow melted first, where vines never suffered drought, where the best fruit ripened (regardless of what varieties they grew). But they also knew that there was a noble grape, and slowly, because they were not under the same pressure as poor farmers and serfs, they could cultivate and protect this noble grape that gave them the best wine.

The Abbey of Cluny was founded by Benedictines in 910 – and endowed with vineyards in the Côte d'Or. But the dissolute life of the Benedictines later resulted in the foundation of the Abbey of Cîteaux in 1098, between Dijon and Beaune, and the strict and devout Cistercian order. They lived by the original Benedictine ethos of *ora et labora* (pray and work), their lives measured in canonical hours.

Pinot's evolution

Tending vines and making wine was thus not just labour, it was devotion and worship. The wine was then used in holy communion, representing the blood of Christ. The brothers and sisters refined the cultivation of Pinot Noir. Their intimate knowledge of sites and the differences between them was accumulated and handed down. This is key to understanding the evolution of Pinot Noir and the identification of hundreds of individual *climats*, or single sites, of the Côte d'Or that today make up a UNESCO World Heritage Site.

Outside this rarefied world, there were no single-varietal vineyards. Instead, there were field blends, where numerous local varieties were co-planted. These varieties were also co-harvested and co-fermented, acting as a kind of insurance that no matter what conditions the growing season held, there would be some fruit to harvest.

These centuries and the slow evolution of both single varietal selection and single vineyards at monastic estates explains what Robinson *et al* attest: "Pinot Noir was already considered to be a variety of utmost quality in the Middle Ages." It is at the same time that techniques evolved to make red wine, rather than *vin gris*.

Historians also believe that Duke of Burgundy Philip the Bold's famous edict of 1395 that decried "disloyal Gamay" and ordered the planting of Pinot Noir added immensely to Pinot Noir's fame and reputation, its *notorieté*. We do not know how strictly this was enforced, but what we do know is that many, many vineyards, donated over the centuries to the church, especially at the time of the crusades when abbeys became large landowners, remained in clerical hands until the French

Revolution in 1789. The land was confiscated and then sold off to those who could afford it – merchants and rich families.

Pinot Noir remained the pinnacle, but it was far from prevalent. The much more reliably and generously yielding Gamay never really disappeared. In 1855, 23,000ha of the 26,500ha total of the Côte d'Or vineyard was planted to Gamay. But this also explains the rarity and esteem of red Burgundy made from Pinot Noir. Everyone over the centuries had sung its praises. Emperor Napoleon himself was a huge fan of Chambertin wines, but the fame reached well beyond France.

Here is Charles Tovey, a British wine merchant, writing in 1862: "The man of taste... will unquestionably rank Burgundy as the first wine in the world." He attests to its rarity, too: "The very first-class Burgundies seldom find their way to England. The quantity produced is limited... Do not believe that the Romanee Conte [sic], or the generous Chambertin, is to be purchased in England, except on rare occasions."

Hard times

But then phylloxera arrived in Burgundy in 1875, causing upheaval. Replanting with vines grafted on American rootstocks, starting in the late 1880s, saved the region – and while the very best estates clung to their fine Pinot Noir, many replanted with higher-yielding Pinots and unsanitary material. Quality viticulture survived of course, but Burgundy did by no means enter a golden age in the 20th century. Economic crises and two World Wars made life and farming difficult. The creation of protected appellations beginning in 1936 was meant to help the recognition and esteem of these ancient vineyards but it is most sobering to read Anthony Hansen's 1982 *Burgundy* book: "Gevrey-

Photograph © BIVB / Denis Gadenne

Clos de Tart in Morey-Saint-Denis, Côte de Nuits

Chambertin, Vougeot, Volnay, Puligny-Montrachet – these and their neighbours are capable of producing exceptional wines. Sadly today they mostly do not, for too much praise has gone to the Burgundians' heads. The fabled quality has almost ceased to exist, even at outrageous prices."

The Burgundy we know today is a far cry from that of the 1980s. The good news is that it has benefited, like almost every other wine region in the world, from advances in viticulture and oenology and a renewed focus on its unique soils and vineyards – leaving the agricultural aberrations of the 20th century behind.

Chapter 3
Burgundy today

Pinot Noir plantings: 12,427ha (30,708 acres)
Percentage of total plantings: 39.5%

The 37-mile stretch of Burgundy's historic heartland of the Côte d'Or, along with the towns of Dijon and Beaune, were classed as a UNESCO World Heritage site in 2015, spanning 142 communes and more than 1,000 *climats*, or "individual plots that are precisely delimited and classified into a hierarchy, gathered around the region's various winegrowing villages", as the Burgundy Wine Board explains.

The hierarchy they mention refers to the classification of vineyards into ordinary vineyards where wines for the generic Bourgogne appellations grow, followed by villages, premier cru and grand cru vineyards. They run along a north-south escarpment of Jurassic limestone, facing mostly east and southeast. Differences in soil composition, i.e. how weathered the limestones are, how deep topsoil is on the limestone bedrock and the proportions of marl, clay or sand, along with aspect, altitude and the presence of *combes*, or lateral valleys allowing airflow, explain the individuality of the *climats*. Since 1936, they have been enshrined as protected appellations under French law.

> **Some of the villages of the Côte de Beaune are more famous for Chardonnay but most of the 33 grands crus are dedicated to Pinot Noir**

The Côte d'Or starts just south of Dijon, and its northern part is

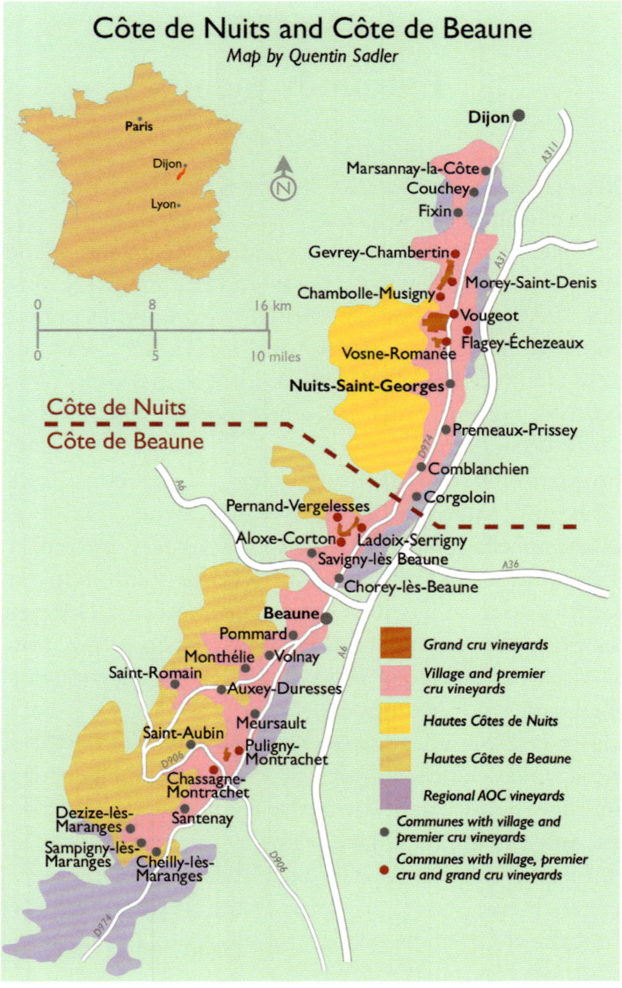
Côte de Nuits and Côte de Beaune
Map by Quentin Sadler
Paris
Dijon
Lyon
0
8
16 km
0
5
10 miles
Côte de Nuits
Côte de Beaune
Dijon
Marsannay-la-Côte
Couchey
Fixin
Gevrey-Chambertin
Morey-Saint-Denis
Chambolle-Musigny
Vougeot
Flagey-Échezeaux
Vosne-Romanée
Nuits-Saint-Georges
Premeaux-Prissey
Comblanchien
Corgoloin
Pernand-Vergelesses
Aloxe-Corton
Ladoix-Serrigny
Savigny-lès Beaune
Chorey-lès-Beaune
Beaune
Pommard
Monthélie
Volnay
Saint-Romain
Auxey-Duresses
Meursault
Saint-Aubin
Puligny-Montrachet
Chassagne-Montrachet
Dezize-lès-Maranges
Santenay
Sampigny-lès-Maranges
Cheilly-lès-Maranges
A311
A31
A6
A36
D974
D906
Grand cru vineyards
Village and premier cru vineyards
Hautes Côtes de Nuits
Hautes Côtes de Beaune
Regional AOC vineyards
Communes with village and premier cru vineyards
Communes with village, premier cru and grand cru vineyards

called Côte de Nuits, running from Marsannay via Fixin, Gevrey-Chambertin, Morey-Saint-Denis, Chambolle-Musigny, Vougeot, Flagey-Echézeaux, Vosne-Romanée and Nuits-Saint-Georges to Corgoloin.

Its southern part is called Côte de Beaune and runs from Buisson and Pernand-Vergelesses via Ladoix-Serrigny, Aloxe-Corton, Savigny-lès-Beaune, Beaune, Pommard, Volnay, Monthélie, Meursault, Chassagne-Montrachet and Santenay to Maranges. Hallowed names indeed.

Some of the villages of the Côte de Beaune are more famous for Chardonnay but most of the 33 grands crus are dedicated to Pinot Noir, while just under half of the 640 premiers crus are Pinot Noir appellations. Irancy is Burgundy's northern outpost of Pinot Noir, very close to Chablis, and Pinot Noir is also grown in the Côte Chalonnaise, notably in Givry, and further south in the Mâconnais.

Highly prized

Pinot Noir's success is evident when we look at historic figures. Across Burgundy, when its entire vineyards amounted to just under 12,700ha in 1958, there were 4,388ha of Pinot Noir. By 2000, this had risen to 10,086ha of Pinot Noir in a total vineyard of 28,447ha. Today there are 12,427ha of Pinot Noir out of 31,463ha total vineyard. This expansion is explained by the fact that Burgundy's wines are the most expensive in the world today, sought after globally. Demand outstrips production by far, not helped by very variable vintage volumes.

Burgundy, once a marginal climate for ripening Pinot Noir, now ripens this variety reliably every year. Things have changed immensely since Hanson wrote 40 years ago that "it requires long hot summers for the red pigments in the Pinot Noir grape skins to develop satisfactorily, and these summers are only seen about once every three years in Burgundy".

Today, the challenge – unless you have a year of biblical catastrophe like 2021 – is to preserve acidity and prevent overripeness in the grapes in the face of increasing temperature and heat spikes. This has led some to suggest that Burgundy is getting too hot for Pinot Noir – and indeed if you gave a Bourgogne rouge from the hot 2020 vintage to a Burgundian vigneron from the 1950s, 60s or 70s, he would not believe that this wine came from the region, so ripe, so lush, so full-bodied it is.

A 2019 study by the European Geosciences Union, Dijon, of historic data spanning centuries noted that "the 664-year-long Beaune grape harvest data series demonstrates that outstanding hot and dry years in the past were outliers, while they have become the norm since the transition to rapid warming in 1988".

I put the question of Pinot Noir's future in Burgundy to Laurent Delaunay, president of Badet-Clément, 5th-generation Burgundy vigneron and current BIVB (Burgundy Wine Board) president. He says: "I think that people who are very alarmist and pessimistic have a very limited local view. Scientists are a little more optimistic. Many grape varieties in their native regions have the capacity to adapt. There are three factors on which you can count: natural adaptation, new clones or massal selections and, probably the most important, practices in the vineyard. There are no simple answers to complex questions, it is always an accumulation of small details."

Delaunay cites just a few instances of viticultural practices that help the vine to be balanced and resilient: improving organic matter and microbial life in the soil to optimise water and nutrient uptake in vines and improve water retention in the soil, mulching to cool soil surface temperature and retain soil moisture, preventing soil compaction, and so on. These practices, however, are not specific to Pinot Noir, they are in the arsenal of enlightened wine-growers everywhere.

He also cites drought-resistant rootstocks that tend to grow deeper roots and make it easier for the vine to reach water. The BIVB is also in the process of selecting new rootstocks that combine lime-tolerance with drought resistance. Then there is the ongoing clonal selection of the ATVB (Association Technique Viticole de Bourgogne – see p76).

Vineyards in Santenay, Côte de Beaune

The grands crus

There is no question that the effects of climate change have led to stylistic changes that challenge what we recognise as 'typical' Burgundy wine. Vintages like 2020 show that some vignerons can make exquisitely balanced Pinot Noir despite record temperatures – but this requires years of dedicated and sensitive vineyard work.

We know that Pinot Noir thrives in California's Russian River Valley, resulting in a rounded, rather full-bodied style of wine. Seen from that perspective, Burgundy is not too hot for Pinot Noir. Various villages, formerly often regarded as too cool to bring forth stellar Pinot Noir, now come into their own – like Pernand-Vergelesses or Aloxe-Corton.

Likewise, the Hautes-Côtes now bring forth exquisite wines – all enabled by climate change. The real question is whether the grands crus are still the best sites for the best Pinot Noir. These sites became grands crus precisely because they enabled slow but full ripening. Their mid-slope position ensured good drainage, the best exposure to sunshine and enough shelter from cool winds. "Do you think that the outlines of the grands crus will have to change?" I ask Delaunay.

"It is a very interesting and key question, very controversial. I do not have an answer," he says, but then volunteers some thoughts. "I have had discussions about this, with Aubert de Villaine [who headed Domaine de la Romanée-Conti from 1974 to 2022]. He thinks, and I have to agree with him, that the *climats* of Bourgogne have shown over the past 800 years that it really is the quality and the differences and the unique identity of each of them that are key. Even if we planted some other grape varieties, this unique identity of the *climats* will stay. According to him we

Pinot Noir ageing in bottle

should not speak too much about grape varieties. What is unique and will never change is our terroir."

While this is a very Burgundian answer, I share Delaunay's confidence in Pinot Noir. The most popular and widely planted clones today were selected at a time when climate was still cooler and ripening grapes was still a challenge. Likewise, most viticultural practices evolved to achieve and hasten ripening. Adaptation in both plant material and farming practices will go a long way towards mitigating the effects of climate change.

Chapter 4
Pinot Noir beyond Burgundy

While Pinot Noir undoubtedly became what it is today over the course of centuries in Burgundy, it was never completely confined to this heartland and was also present in several regions of northern France. It may well have travelled with the Cistercians, a new order founded at the Abbey of Cîteaux in 1098. One of its first filiations, in 1115, was Clairvaux Abbey near Bar-sur-Aube in southern Champagne, headed by a young nobleman, Bernard of Clairvaux (1090-1153) who had joined the order at Cîteaux in 1113. He became the most influential of all Cistercians: by the time of his death 344 Cistercian monasteries had been founded throughout Europe and most of them, where climate permitted, made wine – even in England.

Numerous monasteries continued to be founded after his death, and this era of international monastic expansion coincided with the Medieval warm period (lasting from approximately 950 to 1250), when viticulture spread far beyond its current confines in Europe. Over the following centuries, it was the reputation of Burgundy that ensured Pinot Noir was included in collections of vine cuttings that were either sent on official business with the remit of starting wine industries in newly created colonies or travelled privately with enterprising emigrants in search of a new home.

> **“In the second half of the 20th century, Pinot Noir inspired a whole new set of pioneers, often mavericks who were ahead of their time”**

The Sanford & Benedict vineyard in California's Santa Rita Hills

Photograph © Sanford Winery & Vineyards

In the second half of the 20th century, Pinot Noir inspired a whole new set of pioneers, often mavericks who were ahead of their time. Yet they had a hunch and an understanding that Pinot Noir truly belonged to those who could coax out its essential nature – possibly more so than to those who had the ready means to establish vineyards.

Richard Sanford, California's Pinot pioneer of the Central Coast, has put it aptly: "There's a magic in Pinot Noir, it's a lifelong pursuit. While Cabernet is in front of grand homes, Pinot Noir is in peasant plots. Pinot Noir is of the earth – there's that part of Pinot Noir that is decay. There's a sort of fleetingness about it, a purity. It's refreshing. It's without clutter."

Global presence

Today, Pinot Noir is a global success story. Its continuing advance in the world neatly tracks Burgundy's own qualitative revival over the past three decades. Just over 30 years ago, in 1990, Pinot Noir was the world's 30th most planted grape, with 41,539ha (102,645 acres). By 2016, this had changed to tenth place, with 105,480ha (260,647 acres). This is an increase of 254% in 26 years. When this statistic is reduced to cooler and temperate regions only, Pinot Noir today is the most widely planted red grape in these climates.

In some countries – Germany, New Zealand and Switzerland, for example – Pinot Noir is the most planted red grape. In others – Chile, Australia and the US – its acreage is dwarfed by other grapes, but there is scarcely a country that does not have some Pinot Noir. It even exists in Peru and Myanmar.

Pinot Noir's global presence just shows how many hearts and minds this grape keeps capturing across the globe. Climate change has already shifted the latitudes in which it thrives, and may do so even more dramatically within our lifetime. But there is no doubt that Pinot Noir will continue to stay with us, as it already has for centuries.

The next chapter of this monograph deals with those countries where Pinot Noir is commercialised readily – which leaves out much of Eastern Europe.

Chapter 5
Pinot Noir around the world

EUROPE

France (outside Burgundy)

France holds further Pinot promise beyond Burgundy – almost always good value and with distinct regional character, too. While Pinot Noir in the central Loire and Alsace can be traced back to Medieval monastic settlements, its arrival in the Languedoc came later. And while Pinot Noir in Champagne is dedicated to sparkling wine production, there are some still reds too.

Alsace

Pinot Noir plantings: 1,745ha (4,312 acres)

Percentage of total plantings: 11%

It was a long time coming, but Alsace has finally emerged as one of the most exciting new Pinot Noir regions in France. Despite the fact that Pinot Noir has had a historic presence in this northeastern region, until recently it was not a serious player when it came to Pinot Noir. With few exceptions that prove the rule, it is only over the past decade that Alsace Pinot Noirs have been able to take their rightful place in the world's Pinot-pantheon.

> **"Alsace has finally emerged as one of the most exciting new Pinot Noir regions in France"**

There are good reasons for this: Pinot Noir was not a permitted variety for Alsace grand cru when the sites were first delimited and the grand cru appellation was created between 1975-1983, or when more grands crus were added between 1985 and 2007. While there are 51 grands crus in Alsace, there was just one rulebook for them all. This meant that the best sites were rarely planted to Pinot Noir – and until the turn of the millennium, before climate change made itself felt so drastically, it was still a lot harder to ripen red grapes.

Photograph © Domaine Barmès-Buecher

Yet there has been a sizeable and steadily growing amount of Pinot Noir in Alsace: 712ha (1,759 acres) in 1982; 1,016ha (2,511 acres) in 1992, 1,540ha (3,805 acres) in 2011 and 1,745ha (4,312 acres) in 2021. Much of it is destined for sparkling Crémant d'Alsace: its rosé version has to be 100% Pinot Noir by law. But more and more Pinot Noir is now made into still red wine – and some of it is world class. Especially the wines grown on the privileged sites in those lovely east- and southeast-facing slopes of the Vosges mountains.

It was a legal change in 2011 that allowed individual rulebooks for the grands crus that gave the starting shot for the inclusion of Pinot Noir as a permitted variety for three sites where applications were made to the authorities: Vorbourg, Hengst and Kirchberg de Barr – the latter two were finally granted in summer 2022. When Vorbourg will be granted is anyone's guess. Over this key past decade, some producers have made unbelievable strides in Pinot Noir and present wines of immense elegance and silkiness. It was worth the wait.

Loire

Pinot Noir plantings: 565ha (1,396 acres)

Percentage of total plantings: 1%

While there is not very much Pinot Noir in the Centre-Loire today – just 565ha (1,396 acres) in fact – quirks of history compel me to mention Sancerre. Yes, what is today a bastion of subtle Sauvignon Blanc used to be Pinot Noir country. Camille Roblin of the local wine board BIVC writes: "In the 12th century, the wines of Sancerre experienced a considerable boom thanks to the production of red wine [made mainly from Pinot Noir]". The Loire river itself facilitated a direct route of transport that helped garner fame beyond the region. A little later, in the 14th century, Roblin notes, Jean Duc de Berry – yes, he of the beautiful *Très Riches Heures* manuscript – judged the wine of Sancerre as the "best of the kingdom", but being a local, he may have been biased.

The fame lasted: "The wine merchant and writer André Jullien (1766-1832) speaks of the red wines of the Sancerre region as 'delicate reds, spirituous and of a very pleasant taste', while the eminent scientist Dr Jules Guyot (1807-1872) noted that Pinot Noir was the 'predominant' red grape and 'makes all the good wines of the Sancerrois'," Roblin reports.

It was the phylloxera crisis that ended Pinot Noir's predominance in the region, as Sauvignon Blanc was recognised as a more reliable grape with equal ability to reflect sites. In fact, when the AOC for Sancerre was established in 1936, it was for white wines only. It was not until 1959 that the Centre-Loire received its first rosé and red appellation.

In Sancerre (281ha/694 acres Pinot Noir), Menetou-Salon (168ha/415 acres) and Reuilly (81ha/200 acres), Pinot Noir is the

Overlooking the town of Sancerre in the Centre-Loire

Photograph © Jim Budd

only permitted red grape, while in the appellations of Côteaux du Giennois (20ha/49 acres) and Châteaumeillant (1ha/2.47 acres), Pinot Noir is blended with Gamay.

It is fascinating to note that centuries of varietal predominance were (almost) swept away by the appellation laws and it is a pity that Sancerre rouge is not better known. Roblin, however, prefers to state it the other way round: for her it means that despite Sauvignon Blanc's success, Pinot Noir was never not planted, and was never forgotten. Today, climate change also makes a difference and helps ripen red grapes. The best central Loire Pinot Noirs are fragrant and elegant – less so in hot vintages – with a fine line of acidity.

Languedoc

Pinot Noir plantings: 3,507ha (8,666 acres)

Percentage of total plantings: 1.6%

Pinot Noir accounts for just 1.6% of all plantings in the Languedoc-Roussillon region in southern France, but it is concentrated in spots that make sense: most notably in the Haute Vallée de l'Aude/Limoux in the Pyrenean foothills. It is altitudes of up to 600m, with vineyards up to 450m, affording a slightly cooler climate and limestone soils, that predestine the area for Pinot Noir. Just 100ha (247 acres) of the 700ha (1,730 acres) of Pinot Noir plantings there are dedicated to the production of sparkling Crémant de Limoux, where Pinot can make up to 30% of the blend. The rest is made into rather elegant still Pinot Noir.

According to Laurent Delauney, who makes wine there as well as in Burgundy, the only difference is the climate. It is land prices in Burgundy and global demand for Pinot Noir that make high-altitude limestone sites in southern France an attractive

Louis Latour's Valmoissine vineyards in the Var, southern France

proposition. Another Burgundian producer, Louis Latour, makes Pinot Noir in the department of Var, also at 500m altitude. There are also significant plantings of Pinot Noir in Hérault – especially where limestone crops up in its varied soils.

Champagne

Pinot Noir plantings: 13,000ha (32,124 acres)
Percentage of total plantings: 38%

With about 13,000ha (32,124 acres), Champagne, of course, is the other great concentration of Pinot Noir plantings in France. While the vast majority is used for sparkling wines, there has been a history of still red Pinot Noir in the region. The fame of Champagne wines predates the emergence of sparkling wines. French King Louis XIV is said to have had a weakness for

Champenois wines – having been presented at his coronation in Reims in 1654 with wines from Sillery, Hautvillers, Verzenay and many other territories near Reims. Were these made from Pinot Noir? They may well have been, since a 1718 treatise on Champagne winemaking declared that black grapes make the best wines.

While Nicolas Bidet wrote in 1752 that the "The Morillon Noir [Pinot Noir] which is used around Paris to make the best wine... makes even better wine in Burgundy and Champagne."

Bollinger's La Côte aux Enfants still Pinot Noir

Photograph © Champagne Bollinger

The villages of Sillery, Aÿ and Bouzy were particularly noted. Today, still red Champagne wine is still made – in vastly smaller quantities than sparkling wines – and sold under the Côteaux Champenois appellation.

Climate change has given this style some resurgence, as seen in Louis Roederer's ambitious Camille bottlings from the 2018 and 2019 vintages. But it is Bollinger's La Côte aux Enfants still Pinot Noir, harvested from the eponymous hillside vineyard in Aÿ, that has carried the still red Pinot Noir torch for Champagne since the 1930s. The Champenois make many red wines of course – they need it to colour their rosé d'assemblage Champagne, so they do not sell it as still red wine.

Germany

Pinot Noir plantings: 11,602ha (28,669 acres)

Percentage of total plantings: 11%

When German Pinot Noirs first emerged in international markets in the late 2000s and early 2010s, they were not taken seriously. The wines were often met with disbelief and ridicule, sometimes even hostility. Robert Parker, at the height of his influence in 2002, famously wrote in the sixth edition of his *Parker's Wine Buyer's Guide* that German Pinot Noir was a "a grotesque and ghastly wine that tastes akin to a defective, sweet, faded, diluted red Burgundy from an incompetent producer. Need I say more?"

He could not have been more damning. How could such a frigid country dedicated to white wine even dream of making red wines? Both wine-drinking camps had

> **"Germany is the world's third-largest producer of Pinot Noir after France and the US"**

SPÄTBURGUNDER

made their minds up: those who had filed Germany as the home of sweetish, unserious and undrinkable plonk – hello, Blue Nun – and those who for years had squirreled away the most precious bottles of finest Riesling, from Kabinett all the way to Trockenbeerenauslese.

Germany's success on the international Pinot Noir scene thus faced a far bigger cultural obstacle than any new or emerging Pinot Noir region elsewhere in the world. Yet, once you put two and two together, all of Germany's 13 winegrowing regions spread across four degrees of latitude are a natural home for Pinot Noir. The climate used to be marginal to cool, now it's temperate. It is continental, providing long autumns.

Germany's soils are as varied as the regions and boast slate, shale, schist, rhyolite, granite, gneiss, loess, loam, sandstone and various limestones. All of them can bring forth great Pinot Noir. On top of that, Germany's choicest vineyards tend to be on gentle to steep slopes of benign aspect, often close to a moderating body of water. So if (an increasingly warm) climate, great vineyard soils and topography make a great home for Pinot Noir – or Spätburgunder as the grape is known in Germany – why did it take the Germans such a long time to make great Pinot Noir?

Quantity to quality

The reasons are found in history: for a long time, Germany was too cool to ripen Pinot Noir reliably in every vintage – as was Burgundy at the time. A more salient reason was attitude: battered by losing two World Wars in which it had been the chief aggressor, Germany started the second half of the 20th century as a rather drab and brow-beaten nation with both its vineyards and its reputation in tatters. With the economic upswing of the 1950s, a new spirit took over and supposed progress became the watchword. Despite a history of world-class winemaking in prestigious regions like Mosel and the Rheingau, a distinct shift took place that favoured industrialised agriculture.

Germany's new wine law in 1971 allowed huge yields and did not distinguish between noble and lesser grape varieties. The only defining quality parameter was the ripeness of the grapes at harvest and whether wines had been chaptalised. Neither did Germany have great genetic planting material – German clones until that time had been bred solely for yield stability. It was impossible to ripen high yields of Pinot Noir in such a cool climate and German Pinot Noir was in the doldrums.

Yet Spätburgunder had a long presence in Germany: there are mentions from the early 14th century, although their reliability is

Vineyards in the village of Assmannshausen, on the Rhine

Photograph © Deutsches Weininstitut

questionable. The trouble with proving a most plausible and logical connection to early monastic settlements who may well have brought Pinot Noir to Germany is a lack of documentation. The Thirty Years' War (1618-1648) was one of Europe's most devastating and calamitous conflicts and Germany provided its chief battlefields.

This war and later conflicts decimated the population and wreaked destruction so that much documentation was lost to siege, pillage and fire. Yet small pockets of Pinot Noir remained in Germany: the village of Assmannshausen in the Rheingau and Ingelheim in Rheinhessen, for instance, and Baden.

In 1926, when there were about 72,000ha (177,916 acres) of vines in Germany, just 2.9% (about 2,090ha/5,165 acres) of them were Pinot Noir. By 1964, there were 1,839ha (4,544 acres), by 2000 there were 9,255ha (22,870 acres), and today there are 11,602ha (28,669 acres) – which makes Germany the world's third-largest producer of Pinot Noir after France and the US.

This resounding success is down to a complete shift from quantity to quality, pioneered by curious winemakers who were fed up with the status quo of the late 1980s and 90s and to their children who drove this quality ethos forward via much better viticulture and sensitive winemaking.

Pinot Noir is present in all 13 growing regions. Baden, Rheinhessen, Pfalz, Württemberg, Rheingau and Ahr have sizeable plantings, while Mosel, Nahe and Franken have less – but no less compelling – Pinot Noir.

Stylistically, it is impossible to pin German Pinot Noir down, but it is safe to say that Germany today offers a scintillating playground for any Pinot-lover. No longer is any doubt that some of them are world class.

Italy

Pinot Noir plantings: Data not available

Percentage of total plantings: <1%

Italy may not be the first country you think of at the mention of Pinot Noir, yet there are substantial plantings in Alto Adige and Lombardy, namely in Oltrepò Pavese. That Italy has an ancient wine culture is indisputable, but Pinot Noir's – or rather Pinot Nero's – history in the country is more recent and today confined to its north.

There is a key figure: Archduke Johann of Austria (1782-1859), a scion of the sprawling House of Habsburg and a reformer and innovator of agriculture – especially viticulture. He brought Pinot Noir to Italy's subalpine north – namely Alto Adige – in the 1830s, alongside other grape varieties, in a drive to improve viticulture and the lot of the local farmers.

The first mention of a quality wine can be found in 1869 and a year later Ludwig Barth von Barthenau planted Pinot Nero in his vineyard in Mazon. Mazon (sometimes also spelled Mazzon) is still a hotspot for Pinot Noir today. "Mazon and Pinot Nero is a success story that began in 1959 and 1960," says Martin Foradori Hofstätter of Tenuta J Hofstätter.

It was in 1959 that his grandfather Paolo Foradori bought the historic Barthenau vineyard whose Pinot grapes were previously used to give a bit more colour and backbone to the classic, pale Schiava-based wines of Lago Caldaro. Possibly the only instance of this use of Pinot Noir. Paolo Foradori thus revived the historic vineyard and proved that Mazon was a perfect subzone for Pinot Nero in Alto Adige.

> **The real concentration of Pinot Noir is in Lombardy's Oltrepò Pavese region**

There are currently 552ha (1,364 acres) of Pinot Noir in Alto Adige, up from 150ha (371 acres) in 1960. Alto Adige Pinot Noirs thrive at altitudes above 400m and its best examples, notably J Hofstätter's Barthenau Vigna S Urbano, have an Italianate lift that combines beautifully with the essential nature of Pinot Noir.

Neighbouring Trentino has 375ha (927 acres) of Pinot Noir, which is used both for the production of sparkling Trentodoc and still red wine.

The real concentration of Pinot Noir is in Lombardy's Oltrepò Pavese region with approximately 3,000ha (7,413 acres) of Pinot Noir. It owes its arrival to the 19th-century fashion for all things sparkling, and was first planted here in 1865 by Count Vistarino,

Photograph © Alto Adige Wine/Tiberio Sorvillo

Vineyards in Alto Adige, Italy

who pioneered traditional-method sparkling wine production in the area – with great success.

Experiments with the first still red wines made from Pinot Noir did not begin until the 1950s – and while most Pinot Noir in Oltrepò Pavese is dedicated to sparkling wine production, it is a mystery why these sparkling and still Pinot Noirs are not better known in the wine world, as Pinot Noir is also capable of great elegance here.

Switzerland

Pinot Noir plantings: 3,802ha (9,395 acres)
Percentage of total plantings: 26%

With 3,802ha (9,395 acres) of plantings, Switzerland is another significant grower of Pinot Noir – in fact, Pinot Noir is the country's most important red grape variety and has a track record with historic mentions dating to 1419 and 1631. But as is often the case with Swiss wines, they are rarely seen in international markets.

Despite being planted in every one of Switzerland's wine regions, much Swiss Pinot Noir (1,358ha/3,356 acres) is grown in the 16 growing regions of German-speaking Switzerland including Basel, Schaffhausen, Aargau, Zurich, Thurgau, St Gallen, Appenzell and Graubünden (Grisons), i.e. the country's north. There are also significant plantings (1,345ha/3,324 acres) in the Valais along the Rhône river, where warm foehn winds help to ripen grapes in higher altitudes – but hectarage is declining in both German-speaking Switzerland and the Valais.

In the Valais, until the 1940s, pure Pinot Noir was sold under the name of Dôle – today this term denotes a blend of a majority of Pinot Noir and Gamay (together they must account for at least

The village of Ardon in the French-speaking part of the Valais

Photograph © Markus Hungerbühler DipWSET

85%). While Dôle is known as an easy-drinking red, Swiss Pinot Noirs can be world class. In the Vaud, where there are less than 550ha (1,359 acres) of Pinot Noir, Oeil-de-Perdrix, a Pinot Noir rosé, is of local importance. A history of clonal selection at Swiss research institutes, especially Wädenswil (today subsumed into Agroscope), means that there are Swiss Pinot Noir clones that still have international importance too.

Austria

Pinot Noir plantings: 589ha (1,455 acres)
Percentage of total plantings: 1.3%

In Austria, where there are just under 590ha (1,455 acres) of Pinot Noir, the grape is mostly called Blauburgunder. It predominates in the Thermenregion, south of Vienna, and has a long track record there.

Some surmise that Pinot Noir got to Austria via the Cistercians, while others note the year 1394 as the first documented planting of the variety in Austria. It also has a presence in Austria's warmest and easternmost growing region Burgenland, where both Blaufränkisch and Zweigelt predominate – benefiting from the warm continental climate of its summers, which are almost too hot for delicate Pinot Noir.

There is also some Pinot Noir in Vienna's own vineyards and some of these are worth seeking out.

Eastern Europe

While Bulgaria, the Czech Republic, Hungary and Moldova, Romania, Serbia and Slovenia also clock up quite some hectarage of Pinot Noir together, these wines are not present in the international market, save for generic Bulgarian or Hungarian bulk Pinot Noir that finds its way into own-brand bottlings of numerous European supermarkets.

England and Wales

Pinot Noir plantings: 1,101 (2,720 acres)

Percentage of total plantings: 29%

England may be the latest arrival on the global Pinot Noir scene. It is no longer news that England is an excellent and ever-improving source of fine traditional-method sparkling wines, but in recent years it has hits its stride with still red Pinot Noir.

While there is evidence of Roman viticulture in England, the Domesday Book from 1086 notes the existence of 42 vineyards, and we know the Cistercians made wine, there was a long hiatus when England did not have a wine industry to speak of.

In the 20th century, this mainly focused on growing hybrids and many German crossings that had been bred to clock up sugar in what Stephen Skelton MW calls an "ultra-cool" climate. Change only came with the impetus of Sandy and Stuart Moss, who were the first to purposely plant vines, namely Pinot Noir, Chardonnay and Pinot Meunier, with the aim of making traditional-method sparkling wines in 1988 at their Nyetimber estate in West Sussex.

This was the move that launched what is now a thriving industry. But still red wine? Skelton notes that there were just 11ha (27 acres) of Pinot Noir plantings in England in 1984 – of a total of 430ha (1,063 acres) mainly made up of Müller-Thurgau, Reichensteiner and Seyval Blanc. Today, this figure stands at 1,101ha (2,720 acres) of Pinot

“Change only came with the impetus of Sandy and Stuart Moss”

Photograph © Danbury Ridge Wine Estate

The River Crouch in Essex, England

Noir, making it the second-most planted variety after Chardonnay in a total vineyard of 3,757ha (9,284 acres) in 2021 (3,690ha/9,118 acres in England, 67ha/166 acres in Wales – not including 2022 plantings). While the vast majority of this Pinot Noir is turned into sparkling wine, climate change and curiosity have together resulted in a small slew of still red Pinot Noirs.

Winemaker Charlie Holland of Gusbourne in Kent says: "Gusbourne first trialled still red Pinot Noir in 2007, our second vintage on an extremely small scale of less than 50 bottles. The first commercial bottling was in 2010." He notes that the "wines were fairly rudimentary then".

It was the hot 2011 vintage that "produced some amazing still white and red wines, perhaps the first inkling of what we could produce", he writes. It was too cool in 2012 and 2013, but in

2014, "by dropping 30% of the fruit post-fruit set, we were able to significantly increase concentration in the wine, which resulted in a platinum medal at the Decanter World Wine Awards."

More recently, however, with its clay soils and dry climate, the Crouch Valley in estuarine Essex in southeast England has emerged as an ideal spot for making still Pinot Noir. The Pinot Noirs made at Danbury Ridge – one of the first to bottle fine wine in Essex itself and put the county on the wine map – will convince anyone of the potential here. Watch this space. Apparently, a few Burgundians are already prospecting.

THE AMERICAS

California

Pinot Noir plantings: 18,671ha (46,137 acres)

Percentage of total plantings: 7%

Today, there are 18,671ha (46,137 acres) of Pinot Noir in California – 20 years ago there were just 6,805ha (16,816 acres) – attesting yet again to the growing popularity of the grape and the growing expertise with which it is being farmed and made. That popularity was given a most unusual boost in the US that led to a veritable explosion of Pinot Noir in California – the *Sideways* phenomenon.

This 2004 movie, based on the 2004 novel *Sideways* by Rex Pickett, was a skewed paean to Pinot Noir, set in California's wine country, wrapped in a perceptive comedy-drama. Its protagonist's characterisation of Pinot Noir clearly hit a nerve with the American public: "It's a hard grape to grow… It's thin-skinned, temperamental, it ripens early, it's not a survivor like Cabernet, which can just grow anywhere and thrive even when it's neglected. No, Pinot needs constant care and attention… Only the most patient and nurturing of growers can do it, really. Somebody who really takes the time to understand Pinot's potential can then coax it into its fullest expression. And then, oh, its flavours are just the most haunting and brilliant and thrilling and subtle and ancient on the planet."

Since then, the acreage of Pinot Noir in California has doubled in Mendocino County, Sonoma County, Santa Barbara and San Luis Obispo and Ventura Counties, and almost tripled in Monterey County. Evidently, all these counties are on California's cool Pacific Coast, now recognised as one of the foremost areas in the world to grow Pinot Noir.

Bien Nacido winery in Santa Maria Valley, Santa Barbara County

Photograph courtesy of Au Bon Climat

Wave of enthusiasm

Nobody has traced Pinot Noir's US presence better than John Winthrop Haeger in his magisterial *North American Pinot Noir*. The fact that early colonial attempts to establish European grapevines on the East Coast had "succumbed to various combinations of climate and disease", not least phylloxera, makes Pinot Noir a moot point: if it arrived "it perished quite democratically alongside all other *vinifera*".

He notes that following the Californian gold rush of 1848, "an unprecedented wave of immigration from Europe" prompted "the first serious development of agribusiness. French and German orchardists and vineyardists seem to have imported many of the major European varieties during the 1850s". Haeger identifies Pierre Pellier, Colonel Agoston Haraszthy de Mokcsa and Charles Lefranc as the personages who may have first brought Pinot Noir to California.

While Pinot Noir was mentioned in numerous instances, Haeger sums up that "Pinot Noir was part of the minitempest of enthusiasm for European varieties that washed over California... It was never excluded from lists of varieties offered for sale, or from hymns to California's potential to grow fine wine. But just as clearly, almost from the outset, Pinot Noir had the character of an also-ran variety: impossible to ignore because of the great wines made from it in Burgundy, but never attracting the same attention that was lavished on varieties from Bordeaux."

Haeger is also meticulous in tracing Pinot Noir plantings of the late 19th century that survived phylloxera and Prohibition and whose original plantings, cuttings or offspring planted elsewhere, now constitute the set of so-called Californian 'heritage' clones like Mount Eden, Jackson and Martini.

Pinot pioneers

Prohibition, imposed from 1920 to 1933, did Pinot Noir no favours. It regained presence after the repeal in the emerging niche category of dry varietal wine – but Zinfandel still reigned supreme in the vineyards. While the US wasn't a big wine-drinking nation, and virus-free material was not available until the late 1950s, Haeger notes that numerous famous names of California all made Pinot Noir wines. Some even focused on Pinot Noir and Chardonnay, such as 1953-founded Hanzell in the Sonoma Valley, while Chalone in Monterey County kept the Pinot Noir spirit alive in the 1960s.

Acreage increased tenfold from 1961 to 1971 but increasingly it was Cabernet Sauvignon that received most of the accolades – notably in the late Steven Spurrier's famous 1976 Judgement of Paris tasting. Despite the presence of some stalwarts, Pinot Noir lost lustre.

But slowly new Pinot pioneers emerged: in 1964, Charles Bacigalupi was the first to plant Pinot Noir in the Russian River Valley, followed by Joseph Swan in 1968, then Joe Rochioli Jr. Richard Sanford and Michael Benedict did so in 1972 in what is now the Santa Rita Hills AVA in Santa Barbara County, followed by Josh Jensen of Calera in San Benito County in 1975.

> **"The diversity of Californian Pinot Noir is immense, both climatically and stylistically"**

In 1973, Davis Bynum released Pinot Noir made from Rochioli's Pinot grapes, and ten years later Burt Williams and Ed Selyem made their first Pinot Noir (also from Rochioli's grapes), when their winery was still called Hacienda del Rio. In 1980, David Hirsch planted Pinot Noir in what is now the Fort-Ross-Seaview AVA. It was also in the early 1980s that Jim Clendenen established Au Bon Climat in Santa Barbara County and Richard Ward and David Graves started Saintsbury in Carneros. This was the start of the New Californian Pinot wave that then received its super boost by the *Sideways* movie in 2004. Since then, winemaking has become more and more refined.

With 800 miles of coastline, and Pinot Noir thriving from the 34th to the 39th degrees of latitude along that coast, on either side of the coastal ridges, the diversity of Californian Pinot Noir is immense, both climatically and stylistically. The interplay between inland heat and cold Pacific air, along with aspect and topography, determine where Pinot Noir does best.

The most exciting developments came with the further exploration and development of cooler and even marginal spots for Pinot Noir along the central and north Pacific coast. These wines have wonderfully bright acidity and seem to combine the scent of the salty ocean with that of fragrant conifer.

Oregon

Pinot Noir plantings: 9,531ha (23,552 acres)

Percentage of total plantings: 60%

Oregon's Pinot Noir history is clear-cut and recent and therefore all the more impressive, especially considering the presence of many Burgundian-owned and -founded estates today. It is all down to two men, classmates at UC Davis in California, David Lett of Eyrie Vineyards and Charles Coury. While viticulture in Oregon can be traced to the mid-19th century, Pinot Noir arrived in Oregon with Lett and Coury in 1965.

The late David Lett spoke and wrote extensively about his and Pinot Noir's beginnings in Oregon's Willamette Valley. He arrived in Oregon as a 24-year-old graduate with a dream of making cool-climate Pinot Noir.

> **"Where grape maturity coincides with the very end of a cool growing season, the wines made from them are the best the variety can produce – David Lett"**

He explained his thinking in a speech he gave at McMinnville in 1996: "Upon graduation from Davis in January of 1964 I sailed off for Europe armed with letters of introduction and a lot of questions. The secret I discovered was really no secret at all – it had evolved empirically over the previous ten to 15 centuries of grape-growing in Europe. Grape growers are farmers and farmers don't normally go looking for more trouble than nature always provides. This perverse bunch of European grape farmers, however, kept growing certain varieties in regions where grape maturity is in doubt almost every year. Why? The secret is that where grape maturity coincides with the very end of a cool growing season, the wines made from them are the best the variety can produce. By the way, this is the same 'secret' that gives the Willamette Valley the most flavourful fruits, nuts and berries in the US – perhaps the world."

Inland winelands

Both the volcanic soils and the Oregon climate suited Pinot Noir. Oregon's winelands are inland, protected from the cool Pacific by the Coast Range, yet there is a maritime influence and, at a latitude of 45 degrees, longer daylight hours, which make all the difference at the end of the growing season. In the 1970s, Lett was joined by further pioneers, the founders of Adelsheim Vineyard, Erath Winery, Elk Cove Vineyards, Ponzi Vineyards and Sokol Blosser Winery.

Photograph © Andrea Johnson

Second-generation winegrower Alex Sokol Blosser outside his wine cellar in Oregon

In 1979, a Pinot Noir made by Lett from the 1975 vintage was in the top ten wines of a blind tasting in Paris – next to the best Burgundies. This prompted Robert Drouhin, of Maison Joseph Drouhin in Beaune, Burgundy, to repeat the tasting in 1980. This time, Lett's Eyrie Vineyards Pinot Noir took second place. Drouhin thus sent his daughter Véronique to Oregon in 1986 to work as a winery intern as part of her oenology degree. In 1987, the Drouhin family bought land in Oregon and founded their winery. "We made wine and we liked it, and we brought it back to our friends in Burgundy. We wanted them to be honest. They liked the wine but thought Oregon was crazy," Véronique Drouhin said in a 2020 interview.

Both Lett and Drouhin had the right hunch. The figures say it all. Official records of the Oregon Wine Board begin in 1981, when there were 404ha (998 acres) of Pinot Noir in Oregon out of a total of 1,238ha (3,059 acres), owned by 80 wine growers. By 2000, there were 1,156ha (2,857 acres), and today there are 9,531ha (23,552 acres), with Pinot Noir representing 60% of all Oregon plantings.

And it's not just the Drouhins who have given their seal of approval to the region: there are numerous collaborations, with the likes of Résonance, Evening Land Vineyards, Beaux Frères and Nicolas-Jay all having some sort of Burgundian involvement. There could be no greater compliment for these nuanced, red-fruited Pinot Noirs.

Canada

Pinot Noir plantings: Data not available

Percentage of total plantings: Data not available

Despite early records – of Samuel de Champlain, founder of Quebec, planting European grapevines around that city in the early 1600s and of a small vineyard planted in Bear River, Nova Scotia by French settler Louis Hébert in 1611 – Canada's wine industry is young.

Pinot Noir only has a tiny presence in Nova Scotia today, with most wines being made from hardier hybrids that can thrive in such a cold climate – across just 404ha (998 acres) of vineyards. There, as elsewhere, the climatic extremes of northerly latitudes are moderated by bodies of water: large lakes and the oceans on either coast. In the province of Quebec, there are just 800ha (1,977 acres) of vines and Pinot Noir represents just 4% – or 32ha (79 acres).

Likewise, in Ontario, Pinot Noir has only a small presence, but it was pioneered here by Karl Kaiser in the early 1980s. In

1975, Kaiser had co-founded the Inniskillin Winery with Donald Ziraldo. They had planted European grape vines in 1974, and ten years later he succeeded in making ice wine, putting Ontario on the world wine map. Kaiser encouraged others to plant and the Lowrey family (Lowrey Vineyard) planted Ontario's first Pinot Noir vines in 1984.

Some of these vines are still in production today – made into wine by the Lowreys themselves, along with Thomas Bachelder. Kaiser himself then also planted Pinot Noir in Inniskillin's Montague vineyard.

Canada's other home for Pinot Noir is in British Columbia. The signing of a free-trade agreement with the US in 1990 – and

Pinot Noir vines at the Blue Mountain winery, Okanagan Valley, Canada

Photograph © Chris Stenberg

a subsequent change in regulations – was the opening shot for a revamp of a wine industry that had heavily relied on hybrid varieties. Pinot Noir went from just 23ha (57 acres) in 1990 to 539ha (1,332 acres) today and is now the second-most planted red variety. It thrives on Vancouver Island on the coast as well as in the inland regions of Fraser Valley, Okanagan Valley, Thompson Valley and Kootenays – and it looks like Canada will become a bigger player in Pinot Noir as the vines mature.

Chile

Pinot Noir plantings: 4,179ha (10,327 acres)
Percentage of total plantings: 3%

Vines have thrived in Chile since the middle of the 16th century – because the Spanish colonisers needed sacramental wine and local settlers were thirsty. And while Chile today is South America's Pinot powerhouse with 4,179ha (10,327 acres), the variety still only represents 3% of Chile's vineyards. But its rise has been steep – up from just 138ha (341 acres) in 1994.

Pinot only started to make inroads as the cooler coastal areas were prospected for suitable vineyard land – initially for white grapes such as Chardonnay and Sauvignon Blanc. Pablo Morandé was one of the pioneers. Employed by Concha y Toro at the time (in the 1970s), he looked for great sites to plant Chardonnay and hit upon Casablanca on the Pacific coast in 1980 – because there was irrigation water available, the lack of which had halted a trial in Leyda a year earlier.

His employers thought this was too risky: "The company didn't want to proceed until there was certainty, which was ten years later. So I embarked on the adventure on my own because I was very convinced," he says. Thus, Pinot Noir only came later.

Morandé dates the first plantings of Pinot Noir in Casablanca to the early 1990s – and these vines are still used as a base for Morandé's sparkling wines today (as reds they did not achieve the desired result).

Production shift

Other coastal areas, such as Leyda, were not planted until the late 1990s. Star winemaker Francisco Baettig, the man behind Errázuriz, Seña and Viñedo Chadwick, points out that things really changed when good, virus-free planting material became available. A real revolution has taken place for Pinot Noir, both in vineyard and cellar, as Viviana Navarrete, winemaker at Viña Leyda recounts: "It has not been an easy journey with Pinot Noir. It was produced very differently in Chile ten years ago compared to today. The wine was made very differently, with more barrel ageing, higher alcohol, greater extraction and structure. In 2014 we made a huge shift."

This meant "earlier harvests, use of some whole bunches, native yeasts and a move away from so much barrel towards fermenting and ageing wine in other vessels that were friendlier to the fruit, such as concrete vats and less-toasted casks. This allowed us to take a major leap forward in quality."

She speaks for a lot of Chileans in this regard. Most of Chile's Pinot Noir is still in Casablanca, but increasing difficulty to secure irrigation water has caused some people to retreat from the region, Baettig notes. Bío Bío also has a lot of Pinot Noir and so have San Antonio, Curicó, Limarí and Aconcagua Costa. But there is a new Eldorado for Pinot Noir in Chile: the Malleco Valley (south of Bío Bío), which used to be too cool, is now carving out a reputation for both Chardonnay and Pinot Noir.

Baettig has started his own Pinot Noir project there – looking for weathered, red clay soils with just the right kind of water retention – while both Navarrete and Morandé are involved in Pinot Noir projects in the area, too.

All are enthusiastic: "The climate in the Malleco Valley is cold and rainy in the winter. Its summers are more temperate and there is less precipitation. The grapes ripen slowly and constantly, moderate temperatures preserve acidity and generate fresh and floral aromas," Morandé says. The results are "surprising, very impressive. It's a dream! The elegance and unique typicity the wines show more than justify the effort". Expect to hear a lot more from this new and exciting region.

The Errázuriz winery in Chile's Aconcagua Valley

Photograph Courtesy of Hatch Mansfield Agencies / Viña Errázuriz

Argentina

Pinot Noir plantings: 1,993ha (4,925 acres)

Percentage of total plantings: 1%

A mere 1% of Argentina's vineyard is planted to Pinot Noir – namely 1,993ha. While this is sizeable and most of these hectares are in Mendoza, the extreme altitude of the vineyards there and the solar intensity is not necessarily the right place for nuanced Pinot Noir, despite valiant efforts by good wineries. It is in Argentina's south, in the regions of Neuquén, Río Negro and Chubut – all in Patagonia – that Pinot Noir absolutely excels.

Tender, expressive and layered wines emerge from these regions, especially Río Negro (37.5°-40.45°S) and Chubut (42°-

An armadillo with Pinot Noir vines at Bodega Chacra in Río Negro, Argentina

Photograph © Bodega Chacra

45°S). At these higher latitudes and lower elevations, Pinot Noir seems to have found a most convincing home. The coolest sites in Chubut are truly marginal and extreme in a different way. Maximo Rocca of Otronia winery refers to the whipping Andean winds that can reach speeds up to 80mph (130km/h), as well as frequent winter frosts and cold temperatures moderated by large bodies of water like Lake Musters, when he says viticulture at Otronia is "at the edge of the impossible".

While most of these southern developments are as recent as the early 2000s, there are earlier traces of Pinot endeavour in Argentina. Bodega Chacra in Río Negro, for instance, farms Pinot Noir vineyards planted in 1932 and 1955. Both are bottled separately and are marvels of purity and freshness. Indeed, figures unearthed by Bodega Chacra note that back in 1964, there were 2,400ha (5,931 acres) of Pinot Noir in Río Negro – more than in all of Argentina today.

Let us hope that these trailblazers in Chacra and Otronia inspire many more to brave these cooler climes.

Australia

Pinot Noir plantings: 4,948ha (12,227 acres)

Percentage of total plantings: 3.7%

Three names and dates are forever associated with the European grape vine in Australia. First, Captain Arthur Phillip, first governor of New South Wales, who brought grape vines to Australia on the First Fleet in 1788. They were picked up in Rio de Janeiro and Cape Town en route from Portsmouth in England and were planted in the grounds of Government House, now Sydney's Botanic Gardens. Efforts to make wine from them failed.

Second, it was in 1815 that agronomist John Macarthur, who first planted vines at Elizabeth Farm, near present-day Parramatta in 1793, travelled to France and Switzerland with his sons James and William, with the purpose of researching colonial crops of "wine, silk, olives and poppy seeds" and "collecting vines and obtaining information regarding their culture".

Macarthur and sons returned in 1817 and established a vineyard nursery at Camden Park, "which became an important source of vine cuttings for the early Australian wine industry", according to Andrew Caillard MW, who is currently writing a history of Australian wine. "There is evidence that 'small black cluster' – or Pinot Noir – was among the vine cuttings, but it may have been brought out as early as the First Fleets."

Third, a young agronomist named James Busby, who had studied viticulture in France and emigrated to Australia in 1824 where he was employed by the colonial government to teach wine-growing, went on a wine tour of France and Spain. He returned to Australia in 1832 with numerous cuttings – which included Pinot Noir, sourced via the Ouvrard family from Clos de Vougeot in Burgundy.

"Some of these original cuttings were planted at his [Busby's] family's Kirkton Vineyard in the Hunter Valley. Vigneron Maurice O'Shea sourced cuttings from these surviving vines and planted them out in 1921 at his Old Paddock vineyard at Mount Pleasant, a vineyard that still exists to this day," Caillard writes.

"During the 1960s, NSW state viticulturist Graham Gregory collected cuttings from these 1921 plantings for the CSIRO (Commonwealth Scientific and Industrial Research Organisation) at Merbein in Victoria. After selection, heat treatment and propagation, MV6 (also known as mother vine 6) was made available for wider planting in 1971. It is highly valued because of its deep colour, varietal fruit definition and concentration."

MV6 has since become Australia's most widely planted Pinot Noir clone. Why is this significant? Because this genetic heritage predates the phylloxera crisis in Europe and, with significant time in Australia, the vine may well have adapted to its new homeland, presenting, if you are inclined to such notions, an 'authentic' Australian expression of Pinot Noir. For more on this subject, see Chapter 7 (p73).

Determination and desire

There are currently 4,948ha (12,227 acres) of Pinot Noir in Australia or just 3.7% of Australia's total vineyard – yet it is a number that has grown steadily. In 2000, there were just 3,223ha (7,964 acres) in Australia. Thus, while hectarage is dwarfed by

Covered vines at Tolpuddle in Tasmania's Coal River Valley

Photograph © Wine Australia

> **Pinot Noir's key hotspots are the Adelaide Hills, Mornington Peninsula, Yarra Valley and Tasmania**

that of Shiraz and Cabernet Sauvignon, Australian Pinot Noir nonetheless is of great importance – because it is planted where it is meant to be and most often made in an artisanal fashion by smaller wineries.

Considering that Australia's wine industry until the 1960s was dominated by fortified wines, it took a whole new set of pioneers to rediscover Pinot Noir in the 1970s and forge ahead in the 1980s. So many names that are famous for world-class Pinot Noir today were not founded until the 1980s and even 1990s and early 2000s – but this tells us that great strides were made in very little time by people who were convinced they wanted to make Pinot Noir, and went to search for the right place to do just that.

Vineyards at the Paringa Estate, Mornington Peninsula, Victoria

Photograph © Wine Australia

The stories of these estates often have one theme in common: the no-nonsense Aussie reliance on science, with land, regions and vineyards mapped in great detail complete with soil and climate data, together with the determination and desire to make Pinot Noir that speaks absolutely of place.

Naturally, we find Pinot Noir in the more temperate reaches of the Australian wine landscape, cooled either by latitude, the cold Southern Ocean or altitude. Its key hotspots are the Adelaide Hills in South Australia, Mornington Peninsula and Yarra Valley in Victoria, and the island of Tasmania. There is more Sauvignon Blanc and Chardonnay in the Adelaide Hills than Pinot Noir, which occupies just 17% of the 3,597ha (8,888 acres) of total vineyard. Of all the Pinot Noir hotspots in Australia it is the warmest, but still a cool-climate region with world-renowned producers.

But it is Victoria – with the Yarra Valley and Mornington Peninsula alongside further Pinot Noir regions of Geelong, Gippsland, Macedon Ranges and Beechworth – that is a real playground for Pinot Noir. More than a third of the Yarra Valley's 2,837ha (7,010 acres) are planted to Pinot Noir.

About 60-70km inland from Melbourne the climate is cool and not nearly as maritime as the Mornington Peninsula, extending south of Melbourne, where no vineyard is further than 7km from the ocean. Just under half of Mornington Peninsula's 976ha (2,412 acres) are planted to Pinot Noir.

"Tasmanian Pinot Noirs tend to be translucent and poetic and as pristine as the island itself"

The climate is also maritime on the island state of Tasmania. Almost half of the island's 2,084ha (5,150 acres) are planted to Pinot Noir – 47% in fact, making it the island's most planted grape. Tasmania, at a latitude of 43°S, is surrounded by the Southern Ocean (to the south and west), the Tasman Sea and the Bass Strait and is thus much cooler than its equivalent latitude in the northern hemisphere. While its western coast is given to temperate rainforest, its centre, south and east tend to be dry, sunny and cool – just made for Pinot Noir. Tasmanian Pinot Noirs tend to be translucent and poetic and as pristine as the island itself.

New Zealand

Pinot Noir plantings: 5,807ha (14,349 acres)
Percentage of total plantings: 14%

Has any other New World country put itself as firmly on the Pinot Noir map as New Zealand has over the past two decades? I doubt it. Granted, I write from a UK perspective, but the US, UK, Australia and Canada are New Zealand's top export markets – more so for Sauvignon Blanc, but its excellent Pinot Noirs are now New World classics in their own right.

This world-conquering prowess is also explained by the fact that New Zealand simply has no choice but to export since there still are more sheep than people on these breathtakingly beautiful islands. The sunny but temperate climate, especially in the south of the North Island and on the South Island are perfect for growing Pinot Noir.

New Zealand's first vines were shipped from Sydney and planted by James Busby – yes, the same Busby who was instrumental in bringing vine cuttings to Australia. He had been appointed 'British Resident of New Zealand' and had arrived in Waitangi – later the site of the Waitangi Treaty – in 1833. He ordered vines and reported in an 1836 letter to his brother that they were thriving, and a few years later his wines garnered compliments. Viticulture existed but did not catch on widely in this far-flung British colony.

The first record of Pinot Noir in New Zealand dates to 1883 when an immigrant Anglo-French couple, William and Hermance Beetham, planted it in Wairarapa, and Pinot Noir was also planted at Te Mata estate in Hawke's Bay in 1892. Romeo Bragato, who became New Zealand Department of Agriculture's chief viticulturist in 1902, had recommended Pinot Noir for planting in an 1895 report. But temperance movements soon took hold and cast their lasting shadow over New Zealand until the 1970s and even 1980s – when the modern era of New Zealand winemaking began.

Early Pinot plantings at Te Mata in 1892

Photograph © Te Mata Estate

The Wooing Tree vineyard in Central Otago

Fine wine potential

The first commercial bottling of New Zealand Pinot Noir was in 1987. Statistics broken down by varietal plantings start from 1989 when there were 138ha (341 acres) of Pinot Noir in New Zealand, this rose to 342ha (845 acres) in 1992, 1,126ha (2,782 acres) in 2000, 3,757ha (9,284 acres) in 2005 and stands at 5,807ha (14,349 acres) today.

The steep growth in plantings shows that Pinot Noir is a key variety for New Zealand. In contrast to Sauvignon Blanc, which has been the catalyst, motor and cash cow of the modern New Zealand wine industry – with currently 26,559ha (65,629 acres) in New Zealand, most of them in Marlborough – Pinot Noir has been the grape that first revealed and now illustrates the fine wine potential of New Zealand. New Zealand has its own set of Pinot pioneers across the islands – not just in its vinous epicentre of Marlborough. They were all on to something.

New Zealand also has its mythical Pinot clone – referred to as gumboot or Abel clone, after Malcolm Abel, a winegrower who supplemented his income by working as a customs officer at Auckland airport. New Zealand has stringent quarantine laws and, in the late 1970s, someone tried to smuggle in the cuttings (in their gumboot) – allegedly stolen from Domaine de la Romanée-Conti's La Tâche vineyard. By sheer coincidence these were intercepted by Abel, a wine lover, rather than some abstemious official. Rather than disposing of them in the incinerator, he saved them, had them quarantined and propagated.

More is more

Most New Zealand Pinot Noir is planted in Marlborough, followed by Central Otago, Wairarapa (home to Martinborough) and North Canterbury. It is via Pinot Noir that New Zealand has been able to tell its story of regionality. This first expressed itself via the difference between Marlborough and Central Otago Pinot Noirs in the 2000s, when Marlborough Pinot Noir, in line with its ethos of consumer-friendliness and approachability, produced fruit-forward, juicy styles, while Central Otago, with its more extreme climate, won over US and UK drinkers alike with its gutsy, powerful Pinots. Much of this was down to viticultural and winemaking decisions that were a hangover from the 1990s and early 2000s when the 'more is more' fashion prevailed in wine: more ripeness, more body, more oak.

What has transpired since is proof positive that New Zealand is a most splendid home for Pinot Noir, because the grape expresses subtle differences in site, soil and aspect. Crucially, these differences are no longer hidden by winemaking decisions or overripeness. Nuance and depth rather than power are the watchwords now. The Maori term of *turangawaewae* – literally translated as 'a place to stand' – has been adopted to speak about this sense of place among New Zealand's winemakers.

And the regional crystallisation has continued: in Marlborough there are clear differences between the warmer Wairau Valley and the cooler Awatere Valley, between clay and gravel sites, while in Central Otago there are clear differences between Bannockburn, Gibbston Valley and Wanaka. The savouriness of Martinborough really shines, while Nelson and North Canterbury bring finesse and elegance in equal measure.

> **"With maturing vine age and an ever-increasing focus on place, New Zealand will continue to be a mecca for Pinot lovers"**

With maturing vine age and an ever-increasing focus on place, New Zealand will continue to be a mecca for Pinot lovers: all the wines seem to reflect both the beauty and the thrill of New Zealand's gorgeous and pristine landscape.

South Africa

Pinot Noir plantings: 1,193ha (2,948 acres)
Percentage of total plantings: 1.3%

South Africa's wine industry was born when Jan van Riebeeck, first governor of the Cape, had vines planted in 1655 in the trading post and colony the Dutch East India Company had established in Table Bay. Pinot Noir itself did not arrive until centuries later. This was down to Abraham Izak Perold (1880-

Aerial view of the Hamilton Russell Vineyards in the Hemel-en-Aarde Valley

Photograph © Hamilton Russell Vineyards

1941), South Africa's first professor of viticulture at the University of Stellenbosch. Jim Clarke, author of *The Wines of South Africa* writes: "It seems likely that Perold brought the first cuttings of Pinot Noir to South Africa in 1910; he was definitely a supporter of the grape, opining that it did well 'even in hot countries', in contradiction to received wisdom then and now."

We also know that Perold made his famous Pinot Noir and Cinsault crossing that resulted in the new grape variety Pinotage in 1924. There were commercial plantings of Pinot Noir in Stellenbosch by Muratie and, later on, in the 1970s, by Kanonkop, Meerlust and Rustenberg. But, as Wines of South Africa notes in its literature: "The variety at the time struggled to take off in areas other than Stellenbosch, because of the strong focus on the production of wine volumes instead of wine quality. The quota system, introduced in the late 1950s, also prohibited production expansions. In the mid 1970s, Tim Hamilton Russell of Hamilton Russell Vineyards in the Hemel-en-Aarde Valley played a huge role in unlocking the true potential of Pinot Noir in the country when he decided to produce the variety in spite of the quota system and the fact that the available clone was aimed at the production of sparking and not table wine."

And unlock it he did. In 1975, he bought undeveloped land inland from the fishing village of Hermanus in Walker Bay and planted the first vineyards in what became the Hemel-en-Aarde Valley appellation in 2009. This ocean-cooled area is now an Eldorado for Pinot Noir. Hamilton Russell made his first

"The red wines made in the cooler areas of Walker Bay, Cape Agulhas, Elgin and Overberg are as compelling as they are complex"

wine in 1981 (I was privileged to taste this wine in 2022 in London – it was still beautiful). His son Anthony Hamilton Russell took over the estate (with his wife Olive) in 1991 and made the decision to focus solely on Pinot Noir and Chardonnay.

In the meantime, Hamilton Russell's winemaker, Peter Finlayson, set off on his own and founded Bouchard Finlayson, just a five-minute-drive away, in 1989, with financial backing from the Beaune-based Burgundy négociant Bouchard Aîné & Fils.

Initially, the success of South African Pinot Noir was hampered by the lack of suitable and virus-free planting material, but this changed in the 1990s. Once again, plantings tell the story: in 1981 there were just 114ha (282 acres) of Pinot Noir in South Africa, while today there are 1,193ha (2,948 acres). Some of these plantings are of course also destined for South Africa's traditional-method Cap Classique sparkling wines, but the red wines made in the cooler areas of Walker Bay, Cape Agulhas, Elgin and Overberg are as compelling as they are complex.

Chapter 6
Pairing Pinot Noir with food

How could we possibly attempt to give food pairings when Pinot Noir comes in a myriad of styles, from innumerable climates and winemakers' hands? We decided to ask winemakers for their favourite pairings. Only one thing is clear: Pinot Noir's immense versatility. Some winemakers were specific with their choices, others more general, and some were moved to muse...

We begin with three specific, mouth-watering pairings: Marie Zusslin (Domaine Valentin Zusslin) in Alsace cites a dish from Marc Haeberlin's 2-Star Michelin restaurant L'Auberge de l'Ill in Illhaeusern: **tournedos of pigeon filled with sauteed foie gras.**

Photograph © Parker Blain / Wine Australia

Pinot Noir is a very versatile food-pairing wine

Sebastian Fürst (Weingut Rudolf Fürst) from Franconia, Germany, suggests **roast saddle of venison with buttered salsify and *trompette de mort* mushrooms**.

But it doesn't all have to be fine dining: Andy Peay (Peay Vineyards) on the Sonoma Coast lets his Pinots resonate with his mother's **bacon and pepper-scented lentil stew**.

Albéric Bichot of Domaines Albert Bichot in Burgundy is "a big fan of relatively young Pinot Noir with **sea fish like turbot, sea bass or bream**. The natural acidity, red berry aromas and elegance all work well".

Francisco Baettig of Viña Errazuriz in Chile loves Pinot Noir with tuna or risotto but also notes two specific pairings: **grilled sirloin steak with *pastelera*** (a Chilean corn dish) and **salmon with shiitake mushroom sauce**.

Jason Lett from Oregon's Eyrie Vineyards, meanwhile, offers sound advice that requires the cook to think: "When you're pairing great Pinot Noir, you are not pairing with a variety, you are pairing with a place. A hard-edged site will bring a hard-edged Pinot, with high acidity and granular tannin textures. For this site, you would want to look for **food pairings with suave textures and generous fat** to enrobe the tannins and release the sensuality of the wine.

"On the other hand, a warm site with fertile soils might give you a very plush, fruity Pinot that would taste flat when paired with something too sumptuous. To bring out the best of the wine here, lean on **fresh herbs and snappy textures** in the kitchen to release the liveliness of the wine."

Paul Clüver (Paul Clüver Wines) in South Africa gives us a whole catalogue of pairings, including **South African *sosaties* (skewers) of lamb with garlic, herbs and spices**, or **salmon with**

Asian nuances of soy, ginger and sake – and numerous other gastro-delights, but he also notes: "The old cliché, that Pinot Noir is a red wine that thinks it is a white wine, still holds true. The

Photograph © BIVB / Image & Associés

combination of red wine and white wine qualities does indeed give incredible flexibility with many different ingredients and preparations to pair them with."

He counsels that anything that is "too bold... overly rich... too hot and fit for fire eaters" or strong-flavoured fish like "anchovies, sardines and mackerel" is not a good idea.

Finally, the irrepressible Nigel Greening of Felton Road in New Zealand delivers wonderful advice and food for thought: "It is said that Pinot Noir has no flavour of its own, it simply acts as a mirror to the place it is grown. Those who say that should get out more; it is very clear that Pinot Noir has typicity of flavour, despite its trick of shape-shifting to reflect its home.

"The simple answer is you start with the soil: the heart of this matter. Foods of the earth resonate with Pinot Noir like no others. **Mushrooms and truffles** are obvious bedfellows. Almost all **root vegetables** want to join the party, but just as Pinot loves to stand alone and shine, the best dishes allow the key ingredients to do the same. Forget complex fusions and sauces that take a weekend to make. Great Pinot dishes make a hero of the **simple ingredients** and allow them to stand up and shine."

Greening follows this with a brilliant discourse on various meats and ways of preparing them (too long to reproduce here) but leaves us with a treasured memory from Domaine de l'Arlot in Burgundy that is a lesson: "The main course was **potatoes.** Not any old potatoes, but Rattes, grown in the premier cru soil right next to the vines of the Clos. They were **slow-roasted with thyme, rosemary and olive oil.** We ate them with our fingers and drank great old vintages. What greater honour can you do to a great wine?"

Clone 777 (top) in ATVB's experimental vineyard in Burgundy, which was photographed on the same day as Clone 115 (above) illustrating differences in ripening and bunch structure

Chapter 7
Clonal talk – Pinot Noir's genetic identity

This rather technical chapter is based on previously published articles written for *The World of Fine Wine* and an article published by *Wine Enthusiast*, summarised here with kind permission of the publishers...

Talk to anyone in the know about Pinot Noir and it won't be long before names and numbers will be mentioned, referring to clones. The talismanic triple number of 777 will crop up, as will names like Pommard, Wädenswil or Martini. Then, usually, somebody will contend that Pinot Noir is a grape variety that is prone to mutation – an erroneous assertion that has been repeated so often that it has almost become accepted as truth.

Thankfully, the academic rigour of Jancis Robinson, Julia Harding and José Vouillamoz in their seminal handbook *Wine Grapes* sets the record straight: "Pinot has hundreds of clones simply because it is very old, not because it is naturally more prone to mutation than other varieties," they say. So why all this talk about Pinot Noir clones? Because they have an influence on yield and growth habit, as well as on the colour, flavour and structure of the resulting wine.

What is a clone?

First, a little background. In viticulture, a clone is an asexually produced vine (a cutting) with identical DNA to its parent vine. Clones are being selected for particular and desirable traits like early ripening, aromatic potential, disease resilience, bunch

"Ever since some Pinot Noir clones were selected for their high quality in Burgundian vineyards, they have become immensely popular around the world"

architecture and so on. Asexual propagation ensures that these traits come true and stay undiluted in replantings.

Born out of necessity, the methods of clonal selection were developed and formalised in the early 20th century. Post-phylloxera, the need for healthy, reliably yielding vines was great. This was achieved by selecting vines with the desired traits and propagating them by taking cuttings, multiplying these in sanitary conditions and making microvinifications to see if the desired and selected traits came true; necessarily a slow and costly process.

Clonal selection was thus mostly undertaken by state-owned research stations who then made cuttings of healthy plant material available to farmers, ensuring economically viable yields. Some private nurseries also made clonal selections and commercialised them. While Germany started this in the 1920s and Switzerland in the 1950s, France did not start selecting clones officially until 1960 – until then private nurseries and growers propagated vines, either by clonal or massal selection, understandably often also focusing on yield rather than quality.

For Pinot Noir, clones are a real talking point as there is such a great variation between clones, down to changes in the arrangement of DNA. The changes between clones can be striking and affect yield, ripening, acidity and flavour. Ever since some Pinot Noir clones were selected for their high quality in Burgundian vineyards, they have become immensely popular around the world with winemakers looking to make quality Pinot Noir.

WHAT'S IN A NUMBER?

The first official French selection led to the release of the first INRA (Institut National de la Recherche Agronomique) clones numbered 111 to 115 in 1971.

This work was continued by Dr Raymond Bernard under the auspices of ENTAV (Établissement National Technique pour la Amélioration de la Viticulture) – hence some of these clones are also known as 'Bernard clones'. Further selections were made and clones released regularly. ENTAV-INRA began selecting not just for health but also for quality and this resulted in the release in 1980 of series 665 to 668 – containing the still popular 667. It was in 1981 that 743 and series 777 to 780 were released, containing the hugely successful 777. 828 was released in 1985 and 943 in 1989 – many of them are collectively referred to as 'Dijon clones'.

Initially just available in France, they were trademarked by ENTAV-INRA and licensed to nurseries around the world, and are now enjoying global popularity. Germany also released clones that were selected for their organoleptic superiority alongside a loose bunch structure and mixed berry size to aid ventilation and prevent rot. These were GM20-13 and FR18-01, released in 1999 and 2004, respectively. Italian and Swiss clones also exist.

What is massal selection?

Another form of selection, also still popular today, is massal selection. This is when a vineyard is observed over years, well-performing vines with desirable traits are marked and various cuttings are propagated as a group, rather than a single plant that is propagated *ad infinitum* like a clone. This method is preferred by some because mono-clonal plantings are in effect monocultures. While they ensure even ripening and even yields, they are not exactly biodiverse. Massal selection is often used to preserve the genetic heritage of old vines and vineyards and is perfectly sanitary if vines are tested for viruses.

The future is an evolution of both methods. The ATVB (Association Technique Viticole de Bourgogne) sells selections, graded as Pinot Noir *supérieur*, *fin*, *fin plus* and *très fin*. *Supérieur* has good, stable yields, while *fin* has less stable yields, and *très fin* has very low yields. While these used to be true massal selections in the past, today they are groups of various proportions of selected clones with known traits that will never be sold individually – only ever in a grouping of either *supérieur*, *fin*, *fin plus* and *très fin*. This is done to ensure more biodiversity in vineyards without running the risk of unknown traits or untested vines inherent in massal selections.

This selection process continues apace and an ATVB *fin* selection ten years ago contained different proportions of possibly different clones than it does today. Why? Because traits like early ripening and lower acid are no longer as favourable as they were in the past. This is crucial and essential work.

Clonal confusion

But there are further layers to clonal talk. The first problem is confusion. Research stations like UC Davis in California or Te Kauwatha in New Zealand with an official remit to support local agriculture also wanted to ensure sanitary and reliable planting material, but their efforts were often hampered by viral re-

TE
PINOT
NOIR
115

Very different leaf shapes at Louis Roederer's experimental vineyard in Champagne

Photographs © Anne Krebiehl MW

ATVB's très fin clonal selection in its experimental vineyard

infection. At UC Davis, one of Dr Harold Olmo's first Pinot Noir imports in 1951 came from Pommard, predating the first official selections made in France. This became UCD 4, its heat-treated offspring became UCD 5 and 6, but all of them have since been struck off due to viral infection. The cleaned-up version is now known as FPS 91. So, when Americans refer to 'Pommard,' they may be referring to UCD 4, 5, 6, or to 91.

Then there is confusion about what constitutes a 'real' clone. Some famous pre-Prohibition vineyards are the origin of both massal selection as well as isolated clones, like the Louis M. Martini vineyard for example. So when growers today speak of the Martini clones, they may have a massal selection from there or one of the selected and tested clones.

A new home

The same is true for other California selections. They are collectively known as 'heritage clones,' supposedly bringing something authentically Californian to a wine because of these vines' prolonged local presence and often mythical past. This is a highly seductive idea when you are standing in a vineyard surrounded by pines, looking onto the Pacific Ocean while sipping some heart-stoppingly beautiful Pinot Noir grown there.

You want to believe that you are not only tasting a wine marked by the local climate, aspect and soil, but by Pinot Noir genetics brought long ago from a hallowed vineyard in Burgundy, now mutated in order to adapt to their new home and thus an authentic expression of the local land. As beautiful as this notion may be, unless the genetics are tested and a mutation is detected, this remains fanciful – which is not to say that the vines in question are not outstanding in this site.

While fallible, there is some logic to this. Since one and the same clone can express itself differently depending on its environment, i.e. a clone in a windy site may have more hairy leaves than the same clone in a sheltered site – known as epigenetic response – many growers observing such differences in the past concluded that their Pinot Noir must have mutated and that they now had a new and different clone. This belief was understandable since the myth of Pinot Noir's genetic instability was peddled endlessly. This led some to believe that their Pinot Noir had a distinct genetic identity and was therefore a newly authentic, local expression of Pinot Noir.

Tracing it back

The history of some clones has been traced. Australia's MV6 clone, for instance, was taken from Burgundy before phylloxera hit. But there are others – all of them propagated from cuttings supposedly taken from famous Burgundy sites and smuggled into the country. They are known as 'suitcase clones'. New Zealand's Abel clone (see p63) is an example of a suitcase clone that was intercepted, quarantined, virus-tested and propagated.

The quality of the planting material and its suitability for a particular site, in combination with the right rootstock, is crucial to wine quality. Availability of sanitary, well-selected planting material – whether massal or clonal – has transformed Pinot Noir's presence across the globe. I also believe that ongoing selection for traits like slower ripening and higher acidity will ensure Pinot Noir's continued presence in global vineyards. In any case, vine genetics are just another fascinating aspect in the endless matrix that is Pinot Noir.

Conclusion

Pinot Noir has been with us humans for centuries – it was, and is, being shaped by our tending, selecting and propagating its most promising vines. Its history is one of human desire made manifest in a grape over centuries of cultivation.

Farming has done this out of necessity with numerous foodstuffs – just think of wheat or apples and their low-yielding origins. But wine in general – and Pinot Noir in particular – were shaped by loftier aims. Just like the drive for beauty brought us the scented splendour of roses over centuries of scouting and breeding, or the sublimation of faith built soaring Gothic cathedrals, the desire for quality, beauty and transcendence brought us Pinot Noir.

> **Pinot Noir is the grape of often bloody-minded winemakers who are as much dreamers as they are pioneers**

Seen in this light, Pinot Noir is a cultural artefact that tells us as much about ourselves as it does about nature. This is where its true fascination lies; this is where obsession is born. Because Pinot Noir is a grape that can thrive in marginal climates, it is the grape of often bloody-minded winemakers who are as much dreamers as they are pioneers. I wish I could tell all of their stories.

We already know in which far-flung places the wilder shores of Pinot Noir are today; we can only guess where the grands crus of the future will be. It almost does not matter where, because Pinot Noir is culture itself – and there's an ongoing desire to express it, in countless forms and in tune with nature itself.

Acknowledgements

With thanks to the many people who provided information, insight and data, listed alphabetically below and with special thanks to Dr Neil Beckett of *The World of Fine Wine* and John Capone and Jacqueline Strum of *Wine Enthusiast* for their kind permission to summarise previously published material.

John Atkinson MW, Foulques Aulagnon, Francisco Baettig, Rosamund Barton, Emma Baumann, Albéric Bichot, Andrew Caillard MW, Gino DiCaro, Liesl and Paul Clüver, Laurent Delaunay, Sebastian Fürst, Linea Gagliano, Nigel Greening, Martin Foradori Hofstätter, Jason Lett, Olive and Anthony Hamilton Russell, Caroline Henderson, Victoria Henson, Tatiana Hirsch, Charlie Holland, Anita Jackson, Kim Jackson, Magdalena Kaiser, Laura Kittmer, Vicky Major, Cécile Mathiaud, Pablo Morandé, Viviana Navarrete, Andy Peay, Léa Riccetti, Emma Roberts, Camille Roblin, Berene Sauls, Jasmin Schmid, Emma Symington, Carlo Veronese, Jo Wehring, Marie Zusslin.

Bibliography

Anderson, Kym, *Which Winegrape Varieties are Grown Where?* University of Adelaide Press, Adelaide, 2013

Anderson, Kym and Nelgen, Signe, *Revised Edition Which Winegrape Varieties are Grown Where?* University of Adelaide Press, Adelaide, 2020

Anstett, Peter R., *Kloster Maulbronn*, Deutscher Kunstverlag, Munich-Berlin, 1994

Austrian Wine Marketing Board, Dokumentation Österreich Wein 2021

Barnes, Amanda, *The South America Wine Guide*, self-published, 2021

Boidron, Robert J., *Le livre du pinot noir*, Lavoissier, Paris, 2016

Clarke, Jim, *The Wines of South Africa*, Infinite Ideas, Oxford, 2020

Deutsches Weininstitut, Deutscher Wein Statistik 22/23, Deutsches Weininstitut, Bodenheim, 2022

Dion, Roger, *Histoire de la Vigne et du Vin en France*, Flammarion, Paris, 1977

Giavedoni, Fabio, "Mazzon, il grand cru del pinot nero in Alto Adige: le migliori etichette in commercio", Slow Wine, slowfood.it, 2017

Gibb, Rebecca, *The Wines of New Zealand*, Infinite Ideas, Oxford, 2018

Haeger, John Winthrop, *North American Pinot Noir*, University of California Press, Berkeley 2004

Hanh, Helmut, *Die Deutschen Weinbaugebiete*, Universität Bonn, 1956

Hanson, Anthony, *Burgundy*, Faber & Faber, London, 1982

Krebiehl, Anne, "30 Years of Domaine Drouhin Oregon", decanter.com, 2020

Krebiehl Anne, "A deep dive into the Pinot gene pool", *The World of Fine Wine*, Issue 67, 2020

Krebiehl, Anne, "Wine Geek's Guide to Pinot Noir Clones Around the World", winemag.com, 2020

Krebiehl Anne, "Cracking the Clonal Code", *The World of Fine Wine*, Issue 55, 2017

Krebiehl, Anne, "How Bouchard Finlayson's Galpin Peak Pinot Noirs age gracefully", The-Buyer.net, 2019

Krebiehl, Anne, "Pinot Noir, A Global Love Affair", *Falstaff Magazine*, Winter Issue, 2022

Krebiehl, Anne, "Santa Rita Hills: Pacific Pinot", *The World of Fine Wine*, Issue 54, 2016

Krebiehl, Anne, "The Extremists of the Extreme Sonoma Coast", *The World of Fine Wine*, Issue 48, 2015

Krebiehl, Anne, *The Wines of Germany*, Infinite Ideas, Oxford, 2019

Labbé, T., Pfister, C., et al, "The longest homogeneous series of grape harvest dates, Beaune 1354–2018, and its significance for the understanding of past and present climate", Copernicus Publications on behalf of the European Geosciences Union, Dijon, 2019

Latour, Louis, *Vin de Bourgogne Le Parcours des la Qualité*, Éditions de l'Armançon, Précy-sous-Thil, 2012

Lett, David, "30 Year Retrospective", Speech in McMinnville on 19 March 1996, EyrieVineyards.com

Lett, David, "On Pinot Noir", Speech at UC Davis on 27 April 1992, EyrieVineyards.com

Lett, David, *Thoughts on Pinot Noir*, eyrievineyards.com, 1996

McIntyre, Julie, *Camden to London and Paris: The Role of the Macarthur Family in the early New South Wales Wine Industry*, History Compass 5/2, Blackwell Publishing, 2007

New Zealand Winegrowers, various annual reports

Oregon Wine Industry History Presentation, Oregon Wine Board, 2022

Oregon Wine Board, 1981 Oregon Winegrape Acreage Survey

Oregon Wine Board, 2000 Oregon Vineyard Report

Oregon Wine Board, 2021 Oregon Vineyard and Winery Report

Parker, Robert, *Parker's Wine Buyer's Guide*, Sixth Edition, Simon & Schuster, New York, 2002

Payne, Alexander, *Sideways: The Shooting Script*, Newmarket Press, New York, 2004

Robinson, Jancis, Harding, Julia and Vouillamoz, José, *Wine Grapes*, Allen Lane, London, 2012

Romé, Helmut, *Die großen Weine Österreichs*, Seewald Verlag, Stuttgart, 1979

Rühl, E., Konrad, H., Lindner, B. and Bleser, E., *Quality Criteria and Targets for Clonal Selection in Grapevine*, Acta Horticulturae 652, 2004

Sagues, Liz, *A Celebration of English Wine*, Robert Hale, Marlborough, 2018

SA Wine Industry Information & Systems NPC, Pinot Noir Year and Plant Year, 1981-2021

Scartezzini, Helmuth, *Erzherzog Johann und der Weinbau in Südtirol*, Südtirol in Wort und Bild No 50, pages 35-42, Bolzano, 2006

Scienza, A. Maffi, M., *Il Pinot nero e l'Olterpo Pavese, Guida all'utilizzo della Denominazione di Origine Pinot nero in Oltrepò Pavese*, Diani & Maffi, Brioni, 2008

Skelton, Stephen, *Winegrowing in Great Britain*, self-published, 2015

Stevenson, Tom, *The Wines of Alsace*, Faber & Faber, London, 1993

Sutcliffe, Serena, *Wines of Burgundy,* Mitchell Beazley, London, 2005

Swiss Wine Promotion SA, *Wine Regions and Wines of Switzerland*, Bern, 2018

Tovey, Charles, *Wine and Wine Countries*, Hamilton, Adams & Co, London, 1862

Vini Alto Adige, *Ausführliche Datenblätter Rebsorten*, Südtirol Wein, 2022

Vocelka, M. and K., *Erzherzog Johann und der Weinbau, Wein in Österreich – Die Geschichte*, Brandstätter, Vienna, 2019

Wine Australia, *Foundations of Australian Wine*, Wines of Australia, Adelaide, 2020

Wine Australia, *The Ultimate Guide to Pinot Noir*, Adelaide, 2020

Wines of Great Britain Limited, *Wine Industry Report 2021-2022*, WineGB.co.uk, 2022